CHRISTENDOM OR EUROPE?

Novalis

CHRISTENDOM OR EUROPE?

☥

Introduction by
Michael Martin

"Christendom or Europe?" is reprinted from
Hymns to the Night and Other Selected Writings,
translated by Charles E. Passage (The Library
of Liberal Arts, 1960); "Spiritual Songs" is reprinted
from *Rampolli: Growths from a Long-Planted Root*,
by George MacDonald (London and New York:
Longmans, Green, and Co., 1897).

© Angelico Press 2024
Introduction © Michael Martin 2024

All rights reserved

No part of this book may be reproduced or transmitted,
in any form or by any means, without permission.

For information, address:
Angelico Press
169 Monitor St.
Brooklyn, NY 11222
angelicopress.com

pb: 979-8-89280-012-9
cloth: 979-8-89280-013-6

Cover design:
Michael Schrauzer

Table of Contents

Novalis: An Introduction 1

Christendom or Europe? 31

Appendix: Spiritual Songs 63

Novalis: An Introduction
Michael Martin

> He was like a bird of passage, tired from its flights over immeasurable oceans, stopping on a green island, and forgetting there its former fatherland, and the vast regions of free thought.
>
> ~August Wilhelm Schlegel

HE GREAT GERMAN ROMANTIC POET AND philosopher known to posterity as Novalis was born Georg Philipp Friedrich von Hardenberg on May 2, 1772 in Oberwiederstedt in Lower Saxony, the second of eleven children, to a family of landed aristocrats, albeit in a period of slow financial decline. Dreamy, seemingly dull-witted, he did not show much promise as a boy. However, after a long struggle with dysentery at the age of nine, during which he nearly died, the young Hardenberg emerged awakened to life and full of curiosity. He applied himself to his studies, relishing in Latin, Greek, and poetry, and displayed a vigor and enthusiasm for life not at all

apparent prior to his illness. A gregarious and open soul, as a boy he loved to regale his younger brothers and sisters with fairy-tales.

Hardenberg took his pseudonym from "*de Novali*," the Latinization of "von Rode," a family name derived from his mother's side. It means "land ploughed for the first time" or "new-cleared land," and embodies the principles to which the early Romantics held—later to reappear in Ezra Pound's credo, "Make it new." This sentiment appears again and again in Novalis's writing. "We are on a mission," he writes in *Blüthenstaub* (*Pollen*). "We have been called to educate the earth."[1]

Novalis grew up in the religious atmosphere of German Pietism and the Moravian Brethren, a religious way of being attentive more to the Christ within and the teachings of the Bible than with structures of ecclesial authority. Pietism was profoundly influenced by the *Theologia Germanica*, by the theology of Johann Arndt, by Johann Valentin Andreae (to whom the roots of Rosicrucianism are traced), and by the writings of the mystical theosopher Jacob Boehme. This atmosphere could also be stifling, however, and Novalis's father was

[1] In Frederick C. Beiser, ed. and trans., *The Early Political Writings of the German Romantics* (Cambridge University Press, 1996), 15.

inclined toward austerity. As a result, the religion of his youth was not able to hold the young man, although the essence of a mystical Christianity remained a quality of his being for all of his life.

Entering the University of Jena at the age of eighteen, Novalis found himself under the influence of the poet, dramatist, and philosopher Friedrich Schiller, one of his professors and a literary giant whom he had long admired from afar. It was then that the young Fritz (the diminutive by which his family called him) became serious about his future as a poet and thinker. Soon thereafter he met the young Friedrich Schlegel, who shared his enthusiasms for poetry and philosophy. The two were later central to the Jena circle that would introduce Romanticism to the world, revolutionizing the arts and philosophy in ways that continue to influence us today. Novalis and Schlegel would remain close until the day Novalis died.

Affable and gregarious by nature, Novalis was charming, charismatic, cheerful, even flirtatious (his brothers teased him as "Fritz the flirt").[2] Tall, slim, and handsome in a nearly feminine way, he

---

[2] Bruce Donehower, Introduction to *The Birth of Novalis: Friedrich von Hardenberg's Journal of 1797, with Selected Letters and Documents*, trans. and ed. Donehower (Albany: State University of New York Press, 2007), 24.

wore his light brown hair long, and his eyes were said to have been characterized by an almost otherworldly fire. Despite his obvious intellectual gifts, he was never arrogant or pompous and maintained an almost childlike openness to others and to the world—which no doubt is the source for the almost universal affection for Novalis felt by those who knew him. He was a voracious reader, an energetic talker, and, perhaps above all, passionate—about everything. As his friend Schlegel observed in a letter to Novalis, "you live, the others only breathe."[3]

Owing to his family's diminished financial status, Novalis had to make a living and, after attaining a law degree, worked for the family salt mines, and later (after studying at the Mining Academy of Freiberg) became a geologist. The spirituality of his poetry found an inspiring counterbalance—a literal grounding—in his researches under the surface of the earth. As he writes in his unfinished novel *Heinrich von Ofterdingen*:

> How quietly . . . the poor miner labors in his deep solitudes, far from the restless turmoil

---

[3] From a letter of May 1793. Quoted in Andrea Wulf, *Magnificent Rebels: The First Romantics and the Invention of the Self* (New York: Alfred A. Knopf, 2022), 142.

of day, animated solely by a thirst for knowledge and a love of harmony. In his solitude he tenderly thinks of his friends and family, and his sense of their value and relationship is continually renewed. His calling teaches indefatigable patience, and forbids his attention to be diverted by useless thoughts. He deals with a strange, hard, and unwieldy power, which will yield only to preserving industry and continual care. But what a glorious flower blooms for him in these awful depths,—and a firm confidence in his heavenly Father, whose hand and care are every day visible to him in signs not easily mistaken![4]

It can be (and has been) argued that the central event in Novalis's short life was his meeting with and subsequent engagement to Sophie von Kühn. And not without warrant. As Novalis wrote to his brother Erasmus on his first encounter with Sophie: "In a quarter of an hour, my mind was made up. . . . It cannot be drunkenness, or I was not born for this star."[5] When they met in Nov-

---

[4] Novalis, *Henry von Ofterdingen: A Romance*, trans. Frederick S. Stallknecht (1842; Mineola, NY: Dover, 2015), 47.

[5] Quoted in Christopher Bamford, *An Endless Trace: The Passionate Pursuit of Wisdom in the West* (New Paltz, NY: Codhill Press, 2003), 204.

ember of 1794, Novalis was twenty-two and Sophie was twelve. By the following autumn they were engaged. Sophie, unfortunately, was never well, and spent much of her short life suffering under the almost barbaric medical interventions of repeated blood-lettings and similar treatments, as well as a number of surgeries—which can only have contributed to weakening her constitution. On March 19, 1797, two days after her fifteenth birthday, Sophie died. Understandably, Novalis was bereft.

Much has been made of the tragic ending of Novalis's love for Sophie, though one has to think that the efforts of his friends Friedrich Schlegel and Ludwig Tieck in marketing Novalis's *Schriften* after his death, and the tendency for the German Romantics to read things in mythic or imaginative terms, contributed to the transformation of a very real human tragedy into a tragic fairy-tale.[6] This is not to say that Sophie's death was not devastating for the young poet. In fact, to say it was

---

[6] This is the argument of Wm. Alexander O'Brien in his *Novalis: Signs of Revolution* (Durham, NC: Duke University Press, 1995), but O'Brien tends toward the sour and whiny variety of literary criticism that the late Harold Bloom listed among "The Schools of Resentment."

devastating is a study in understatement. His thoughts were dark and, while avoiding suicide, he wondered how, like some sort of magician from legend, he might sublimate himself to pure spirit in order that he might rejoin Sophie in the hereafter. No doubt this psychological state was exacerbated by his dear brother Erasmus's death just weeks after Sophie's—and on Good Friday, no less! This constellation of griefs resulted in one of the most beautiful and haunting works of German Romanticism, Novalis's *Hymnen an die Nacht*, known in English as *Hymns to the Night*.

Hymns to the Night is not only a great flowering of German Romanticism, it is a watershed moment in poetics writ large. Like his contemporary, Friedrich Hölderlin, Novalis abandons allegiance to poetic norms and disciplines, breaks all the rules, writing now verse, now prose poems, combining Christian myth, philosophical intuition, and autobiography in a tour de force of Romantic imagination, as if one form alone could not contain the universe he wishes to build. In the sequence of the *Hymns*, Sophie's image is at times clear, at times obscure; it coalesces now with the image of the Virgin Mary, now with the Divine Sophia he found in Jacob Boehme and John Pordage, now with Raphael's painting *The*

Sistine Madonna.[7] The *Hymns* are both an exhilarating and an intoxicating immersion in poetic beauty—a space in which *eros* and *thanatos* are united in a spiritual wedding:

> Praise the world queen, the higher messenger of a holy word, a nurse of blessed love—she sends me you—for I'm yours and mine—you called the Night to life for me,—humanized me—tear my body with spirit fire, so I can mix with you more inwardly, airily, and then the wedding night will last forever.[8]

More than anything, though, the *Hymns* are a work of mourning, a concept to which we will return.

In time, Novalis's soul began to heal. He threw himself into his work as a geologist, finished his studies at Freiberg, returned to writing, and, at last, to life. He even found love again, and by autumn of 1799 was engaged to twenty-two-year-old Julie von Charpentier, the daughter of one his professors at Freiberg.

---

[7] Novalis had seen the painting in Dresden by at least August of 1799. See Alexander J.B. Hampton, *Romanticism and the Re-Invention of Modern Religion: The Reconciliation of German Idealism and Platonic Realism* (Cambridge University Press, 2019), 187.

[8] Novalis, *Hymns to the Night*, trans. Dick Higgins, rev. (New Paltz, NY: McPherson & Company, 1984), 13.

Novalis: An Introduction

But that marriage, too, would never be realized in this world. Novalis had contracted tuberculosis (one can only imagine the effect of spending so much time deep in the cold, damp earth) and moved ever closer to death. In the late summer of 1800 Novalis's health took a turn for the worse. His parents took him to a round of doctors in Dresden, which helped but little. Then, in November, his thirteen-year-old brother Bernhard drowned in the River Saale. Novalis, always close to his siblings, was traumatized by the tragedy, and in his sorrow experienced a violent hemorrhage, coughing up copious amounts of blood. He never recovered.

Somehow, Novalis persisted through the winter, but by March 1801 all knew the inevitable was drawing near. On March 23rd Friedrich Schlegel arrived, and was stunned by the morbid condition of his beloved friend. He stayed at Novalis's bedside for the next two days.

On March 25th, the Feast of the Annunciation, Novalis awoke and was able to eat a little, even to read. But he started to decline rapidly. Still early in the morning, he asked his brother Karl to play the piano while he rested. Novalis slept, his breathing labored and irregular; sometimes he mumbled incoherently. Then, just after noon, he died. As

Schlegel wrote to his brother, August Wilhelm, "Really, it's impossible to believe what a gentle, beautiful death it was."[9] Novalis was twenty-eight years old.

Romanticism and Religion

A primary, if often overlooked, aspect of Romanticism lies in its relationship to religion, and to a reimagined Christianity in particular. Indeed, one might argue that religion is the inevitable *telos* of Romanticism, both in its rejection of the sterile and utilitarian promises of the Enlightenment and in its embrace of the imagination and the call to Beauty. With the English Romantics, this is obvious in Blake and Coleridge, but is also implicit in Keats, in Wordsworth, and (despite the blindness of many of his critics) in Shelley. German Romanticism's fascination with religion was likewise a feature of the English Romantics, right from the beginning.

The Jena circle, to which Novalis was an important contributor, was particularly enthusiastic about a reimagined Christianity. As Dorothea Schlegel wrote in a letter to Friedrich Schleierma-

---

[9] Letter of March 27, 1801. In Wulf, *Magnificent Rebels*, 277.

cher, "Christianity is the order of the day here."[10] Schleiermacher, whose *On Religion: Speeches to Its Cultured Despisers* is a landmark of early Romantic theology, argued on behalf of a Christian intuition implicit in nature and art as opposed to a received body of dogmas and practices having more in common with scientific laws and mathematical theories than with an individual's personal experiences of divinity. "Hence it comes that, from of old," he writes,

> all truly religious characters have had a mystical trait, and that all imaginative natures, which are too airy to occupy themselves with solid and rigid world affairs, have at least some stirrings of piety. This is the character of all the religious appearances of our time; from those two colours, imagination and mysticism, though in various proportions, they are all composed. Appearances, I say, because, in this state of things, more is scarcely to be expected.[11]

Schleiermacher's claim here supports Alexander Hampton's assertion that for the early German

---

[10] Quoted in Wulf, as above, 243.

[11] Friedrich Schleiermacher, *On Religion: Speeches to Its Cultured Despisers*, trans. John Oman (New York: Harper & Brothers, Publishers, 1958), 132–33.

Romantics, "the traditional language of religious transcendence no longer spoke to an age that thought and understood in a language of immanence."[12] Schleiermacher and his contemporaries anticipated by over two hundred years Karl Rahner's observation that "The Christian of the future will be a mystic or will not exist at all."[13]

The "language of immanence" spoken by the Romantics bears of course many resonances with pantheism and panentheism. The Shelley of "Ode to the West Wind," the Wordsworth of the "Prelude," and Blake most succinctly in the preface to *Milton* (known more popularly in Hubert Perry's setting of the hymn "Jerusalem"), all emblematize ways in which divinity informs landscapes of human flourishing. A belief in the omnipresence and immanence of God would not on the surface suggest heresy—or even atheism, as some have suggested—but it does lead to an existential moment in which, if God is truly immanent in Creation, "present equally within everyone alike, then we all have equal access to him, and there is

---

[12] Hampton, *Romanticism and the Re-Invention of Modern Religion*, 52.

[13] Karl Rahner, *The Mystical Way in Everyday Life: Sermons, Prayers, and Essays*, trans. and ed. by Annemarie S. Kidder (Maryknoll, NY: Orbis Books, 2010), xviii.

no need for a religious or political elite to establish and confirm our relationship with him."[14] This last, apparently, was one heresy too many for those charged with the task of gate-keeping the very sacred relationship between the individual soul and God.

Such views brought some of the early Romantics into conflict with ecclesial authority, which, had it occurred a little more than a century earlier might well have resulted in their being burned as heretics. Still, things got hot enough in Germany, in particular for Johann Gottleib Fichte after he published "On the Ground of Our Belief in a Divine World-Governance" (1798), which was confiscated by the authorities in Saxony and eventually led to his dismissal as a professor at the University of Jena. Friedrich Schelling's evolutionary pantheism would later similarly provoke the wrath of the local branches of the world governance in several German cities.

But perhaps even more unnerving to the contemporary ecclesial and political structures (whether Catholic or Protestant) was the inherent

---

[14] Frederick C. Beiser, Introduction, *The Early Political Writings of the German Romantics* (Cambridge: Cambridge University Press, 1996), xx.

activism and chiliasm of these various Romantic "theologies"—however couched in poetic or philosophical language (and often both) they may have been. The Romantics, that is, were not content to postpone the coming of the Kingdom of God to some obscure futurity, but to manifest the Kingdom in the present.

For Novalis, this activism and chiliasm is at its core a magical act. "This new religion," Friedrich Schlegel had written to Novalis, "must be entirely *magic*." And as Andrea Wulf observes, "No, they were not joking."[15] In one of the fragments, entitled "Theosophy," Novalis elaborates:

> We must seek to become magicians in order to be able to be truly moral. The more moral, the more harmonious with God—the more divine—the more bound to God. Only through the moral sense does God become perceptible to us.—The moral sense is the sense for existence, without external stimulation—the sense for covenant—the sense for freely chosen, yet found, and thus common life—and being—the sense for thing-in-itself—the true sense for divining.[16]

---

[15] Andrea Wulf, *Magnificent Rebels*, 243.
[16] Quoted in Jack Forstman, *A Romantic Triangle: Schleiermacher and Early German Romanticism* (Missoula, MT: Scholars Press, 1977), 42.

Novalis: An Introduction

This is a clear example of what Novalis meant by *romanticizing*, the magical act by which the ideal becomes real:

> The world must be romanticized. Then one will again find the original sense. Romanticizing is nothing more than a qualitative involution. In this operation the lower self is identified with a better self. In this same manner we are such a qualitative series of powers. This operation is still completely unknown. When I give the commonplace a higher meaning, the customary a mysterious appearance, the known the dignity of the unknown, the finite the illusion of the infinite, I romanticize it. The operation is the converse for the higher, unknown, mystical, and infinite; through this connection it becomes logarithimized. It receives a customary expression. Romantic philosophy. *Lingua romana.* Reciprocal elevation and debasement.[17]

The ethos Novalis outlines here as the role of the poetic imagination is succinctly articulated by Jean Wahl as a process by which "*Le mystériuex est ici tout près; et l'ici-tout-près est mystériuex*"[18] ("The

---

[17] *The Early Political Writings of the German Romantics*, 85.

[18] Jean Wahl, "La Poésie comme Exercice Spirituel" in *Poésie, Pensée, Perception* (Paris: Calmann-Lévy, 1948), 17–19, at 18.

mysterious is here very near, and the here-very-near is mysterious.") And it is easy to see how much in agreement Novalis would be with Shelley's conclusion that "Poets are the unacknowledged legislators of the world." This is an intuition that undergirds Novalis's "Christendom or Europe."

Europa

On November 14, 1799 Novalis read a new work to some of his friends of the Romantic circle in Jena, including August and Caroline Schlegel, Friedrich and his lover, Dorothea Veit, as well as Schelling and Tieck, among others. The essay, which he simply titled "Europa," created an uproar even before he had finished reading.

Novalis intended for the essay to be published in the *Athenaeum*, the journal founded by August Schlegel and which acted as the mouthpiece of early Romanticism, but some of the circle were aghast at the seeming reactionary medievalism they read in the text and its apparent affirmation of Roman Catholicism—though those philosophical commitments are not really a feature, either of the essay or of Novalis's worldview. The reading even inspired Schelling to immediately pen a hedonistic Epicurean parody of Novalis's piece.

Novalis: An Introduction

The idea was floated of publishing both "Europa" and Schelling's poetic parody of it alongside each other in the journal, but some of the circle were dead-set against publishing Novalis's romanticization of medieval Christendom, no matter what the context. Still uncertain whether to publish the essay or not, the young Romantics appealed to their spiritual father, Goethe, who, after careful deliberation, recommended against publishing—not so much owing to the alleged reactionary elements of the religious vision offered by Novalis as on account of the anarcho-Christian and antinomian strains in the essay. On the heels of the troubles ignited by Fichte's "On the Ground of Our Belief in a Divine World-Governance" not even a year earlier, Goethe thought it best to avoid shaking up the hornet's nest of censorship again with "Europa." But that was hardly the end of the matter.

After Novalis's death, as Tieck and Friedrich Schlegel were preparing the publication of the first edition of his *Schriften*, they included only fragments of the "Europa" essay. It was not until the fourth edition of 1826, however, that the publisher, Georg Reimer, included it—only to have it removed by Tieck in the fifth edition. The subsequent history of the essay has been similarly erratic, with critics interpreting it as everything from proto-fascist fairy-tale to leftist critique of modernity to document of visionary cosmopolitanism.[19] But *"Die Christenheit oder Europa"* ("Christendom or Europe")—the name given the essay by its editors after Novalis's death—is too important a work to be dismissed by such ideological reductionism. For one, it is, like *Hymnen an die Nacht*, a work of mourning, while it is simultaneously a call to a future renewal and regeneration of religion, culture, and civic life. As Gianni Vattimo writes in *After Christianity* (a work that takes "Christendom or Europe" as its starting-point): "One might say, against all narrowly lay expectations, that the renewal of civic life in the Western world in the epoch of multiculturalism is mainly a problem of the renewal of the religious life."[20]

A Work of Mourning

Rather than a nostalgic fairy-tale for a Christendom that never was, "Christendom or Europe" is

---

[19] Pauline Kleingeld, "Romantic Cosmopolitanism: Novalis's 'Christianity or Europe,'" *Journal of the History of Philosophy*, vol. 46, no. 2 (2008): 269–84, at 270–71.

[20] Gianni Vattimo, *After Religion*, trans. Luca D'Isanto (New York: Columbia University Press, 2002), 102.

instead a work mourning the loss of the Christian imagination. The Middle Ages, then, becomes the symbol for that loss. As almost every critic has remarked, the essay has very little to do with actual historical truth. Novalis knew this as well as anyone, which is why he embarks on the romanticization of medieval Christendom as a way to counter the poisonous effects of both the Enlightenment and the Protestant Reformation.

Prior to writing the essay, Novalis had been reading his friend Schliermacher's recent (and anonymously published) *On Religion: Speeches to Its Cultured Despisers*, as well as immersing himself in a deep study of the works of Jacob Boehme.[21] Both nourished his already awakened intuition concerning a fundamental lack in the Christian thinking of his age, a lack that more and more reduced Christianity, whether Protestant or Catholic, to a set of proposals having more to do with political than with spiritual realities. As he writes in the essay: "Protestantism shows us no great and splendid manifestation of the supernatural anymore. . . . With the Reformation, Christen-

---

[21] Paola Mayer, *Jena Romanticism and Its Appropriation of Jakob Böhme: Theosophy, Hagiography, Literature* (Montreal: McGill-Queen's University Press, 1999), 79.

dom came to an end."[22] Moreover, in words eerily applicable to our own cultural moment, Novalis's critique of the Enlightenment is equally scathing:

> Everywhere the sense for the holy suffered from the manifold persecutions of its previous form, its former personality. The end product of the modern manner of thinking was termed "philosophy," and under that head was reckoned everything that was opposed to the old, hence primarily every objection against religion. The initial personal hatred of the Catholic faith passed gradually over into hatred of the Bible, of the Christian faith, and finally, of religion in general. Still further, the hatred of religion extended itself quite naturally and consistently to all objects of enthusiasm. It made imagination and emotion heretical, as well as morality and the love of art, the future and the past.[23]

This is the essence of the mourning that characterizes "Christendom or Europe." It is a lament over what has been lost and destroyed. In this, Novalis embodies what Martin Heidegger describes when he writes that "To be a poet in a destitute time means to attend, singing, to the trace of the fugi-

[22] See page 41.
[23] See pages 45–46.

tive gods."[24] Novalis, like Hölderlin, was nothing if not a poet in a destitute time. The proof Novalis provides of this is that the collapse of Christendom led to the rise of the modern state, wherein "individual powerful states sought to take over the vacant universal Chair, which had been transformed into a throne."[25]

The Regeneration of Christendom

In his holographic poetic vision, Novalis looks not only to the past, but to the future—his as well as our own. That is, for Novalis, the Golden Age "is figured as both past *and* future."[26] But the import of this vision is lost on most critics. The point is that Novalis's "magic idealism" (his term) points to a *kairotic* reality, the reality of the *kairos*. And, in that respect, his vision is utterly and thoroughly Christian.

One aspect of the Christian regeneration Novalis holds up as an ideal is in his evocation of the Divine Feminine, an intuition that he had come to early, but that could only have been bolstered

---

[24] Martin Heidegger, *Poetry, Language, Thought*, trans. Albert Hofstadter (New York: Harper & Row, 1971), 94.

[25] See page 42.

[26] O'Brien, *Novalis: Signs of Revolution*, 233.

by his recent immersion in Boehme. "They preached solely love for the holy and wondrously beautiful Lady of Christendom," he writes in the second paragraph of the essay,

> who, endowed with divine powers, was prepared to rescue any believer from the most dread perils. They told of celestial persons long since dead who, by virtue of adherence and loyalty to that Blessed Mother and to her divine and benevolent Child, withstood the temptation of the earthly world and achieved honors and had now become protective and beneficent powers to their living brethren, willing helpers in tribulation, intercessors for human infirmities, and efficacious friends of mankind before the heavenly throne.[27]

In language similar to that which he employs in *The Disciples at Sais* and *Heinrich von Ofterdingen*, Novalis associates the disclosure of Sophia as an indispensable precursor to the imminent Christian regeneration:

> Whoever has felt it, no longer doubts of the era's coming, and with sweet pride in his contemporaneity steps forth even from among the multitude to the new band of disciples. He has made a new veil for the Holy One, which,

[27] See pages 32–33.

clinging, betrays the heavenly mold of her limbs and yet conceals her more decorously than any other. The veil is to the virgin what the mind is to the body, its indispensable organ, whose folds are the letters of her sweet annunciation. The infinite play of the folds is a cipher-music, for speech is too wooden and too insolent for the virgin: her lips open only for song.[28]

Of course, such language has called Novalis's orthodoxy into question (not that he ever claimed to be orthodox in his beliefs) and caused Karl Barth, a very sensitive reader of Novalis, to observe of Novalis's theology, "Will it be Mary or will it be Christ—Novalis sang the praise of both of them—who will keep the central position?"[29] Barth interprets Novalis as tending toward the Virgin, which, despite his admiration for the poet, causes him no little discomfort and disappointment.

Attending this Sophianic renewal in "Christendom or Europe" is the implicit chiliasm in which so much of the Romantic religious imagination participates. But the way forward is not the way

[28] See page 55.
[29] Karl Barth, *Protestant Theology in the Nineteenth Century: Its Background and History* (1959; reprint, Grand Rapids, MI: William B. Eerdmans Publishing Company, 2002), 333.

back—as important as tradition may be. For Novalis, neither the Catholic Church nor the myriad varieties of Protestantism have much to offer in their current forms:

> The old Papacy lies in its grave and Rome for the second time has become a ruin. Shall Protestantism not cease at last and make way for a new, enduring Church? The other continents await Europe's reconciliation and resurrection in order to join with it and become fellow-citizens of the heavenly kingdom.[30]

One might pause to think that the current state of the West, unmoored from its venerable traditions and in ethical and spiritual ruins, may have lost its opportunity for regeneration. Novalis was fully aware of this, yet spoke nonetheless in prophetic terms:

> Christendom must come alive again and be effective, and, without regard to national boundaries, again form a visible Church which will take into its bosom all souls athirst for the supernatural, and willingly become the mediatrix between the old world and the new.[31]

---

[30] See page 61.
[31] See pages 61–62.

Drawing on Joachim of Fiore and anticipating William Blake, Novalis announces that the Kingdom of Heaven is always already at hand.

Christianity or *Europe?*

After the European Union was formed, one of the important tasks set before its leaders was to create a symbolic representation that accurately depicted the aims of this new allegiance. On the surface, this may not appear as important as matters of policy; but as imaginative act, as magical idealism, it is all-important. The seal, a blue field with a circle of twelve stars, is intended to represent unity; but it is not far, in the language of symbolism, from the "woman clothed with the sun, with the moon under her feet and a crown of twelve stars on her head" (Revelation 12:1). Clearly, the ghost of Christendom haunts the EU, but it can hardly be called a Christian federation. Nevertheless, the Charlemagne Prize, awarded by the EU for "Distinguished service on behalf of European unification" is presented each year on the Feast of the Ascension, though among its many worthy recipients have appeared not a few war criminals. But a man cannot serve two masters.

Can a secular Europe, albeit one around which lingers still the spectre of Christendom, even survive *as* European? This question lurks on every page of "Christendom or Europe." For John Milbank and Adrian Pabst, the answer is a categorical "no":

> An aggressively secular Europe simply has no future, not for Christians, not for Jews, not for Muslims, not for anyone . . . you actually need Christianity in order to uphold a genuine form of pluralism—not a formalistic pluralism of rights or contracts, but a substantive pluralism which ensures that people feel they are respected in their own relational identity.[32]

Or to put it even more directly, "Without the Church there is no way in which Europe can really thrive."[33]

And yet, an aggressively secular Europe is precisely what we have, despite the palimpsest of Christendom over which it has been inscribed. Novalis thought that "from a holy womb of a venerable European Council shall Christendom arise"—but it is clear that the EU is no such coun-

---

[32] John Milbank and Adrian Pabst, "Society and the Church Beyond Liberalism: The Question of Europe," *Radical Orthodoxy: Theology, Philosophy, Politics*, Vol. 3, No. 2 (June 2017): 29–41, at 33.

[33] Ibid., 32.

cil. Nevertheless, Novalis, like his English contemporary Blake, believed that a new, regenerated Christendom must arrive in "the sacred time of endless peace when the new Jerusalem will be the capital of the world."[34] The regeneration of Christendom, as Novalis outlines it in "Christendom or Europe," is nothing if not an act of magical idealism, in which we are all invited to participate. This is the centerpiece of Novalis's Christian Romanticism.

Conclusion

In the second edition of his *On Religion*, published in 1806, Schleiermacher added a passage in honor of his by that time deceased friend Novalis in a section discussing the role of art in religion:

> In place of all else I would point to another example which should be well known to you all. I would point in silence—for pain that is new and deep has no words. It is that superb youth, who has too early fallen asleep, with whom everything his spirit touched became art. His whole contemplation of the world was forthwith a great poem. Though he had scarce more than struck the first chords, you must associate him with the most opulent

[34] See page 62.

> poets, with those select spirits who are as profound as they are clear and vivacious. See in him the power and enthusiasm and the caution of a pious spirit, and acknowledge that when the philosophers shall become religious and seek God like Spinoza, and the artists be pious and love Christ like Novalis, the great resurrection shall be celebrated for both worlds.[35]

Writing over a hundred years later, Karl Barth observed that, of all of the German Romantics, only Novalis "goes on seeming relevant and new" and that "we shall only be able to speak of a true Neo-romanticism for all time when Romanticism is once again seriously taken up in the sense that Novalis understood it and in his spirit."[36] One can only hope that such a time has arrived.

The gift of Novalis's Christian Romanticism resides precisely in his courage to venerate the past while invoking the future. Only the imagination has the power to work this rough magic, and only by being imbued with Christ and Sophia can this imagination achieve life. But this will not happen without the enlivening of the human will

---

[35] Friedrich Schleiermacher, *On Religion: Speeches to Its Cultured Despisers*, 41.

[36] Karl Barth, *Protestant Theology in the Nineteenth Century*, 330–31.

and feeling. We inhabit time thinking it chronos, when, in reality, time is kairotic. As Novalis writes in the last of the *Spiritual Songs*:[37]

> In countless pictures I behold thee,
>   O Mary, lovelily expressed;
> But of them all none can unfold thee
>   As I have seen thee in my breast.
> I only know this world's loud splendour
>   Since then has like a dream o'erblown;
> And that a heaven, for words too tender.
>   My peaceful spirit fills alone.

The regeneration of Christendom, then, as magical idealism, as kairotic reality, is always already happening. Novalis's Christian Romanticism offers us both a method and a *telos* for this great project of redemption by which we further the work of Christ and Sophia in the world. In that, we are all birds of passage.

---

[37] The *Spiritual Songs* are included in this Angelico Press edition as an appendix.

Christendom or Europe?

ONCE THERE WERE FINE, RESPLENDENT times when Europe was a Christian land, when one Christendom occupied this humanly constituted continent. One great common interest united the remotest provinces of this broad spiritual realm. Without great worldly possessions, one Head guided and unified the great political forces. A numerous guild to which everyone had access stood directly beneath him and carried out his behests and strove with zeal to confirm his beneficent power. Every member of this organization was universally honored, and if the common people sought comfort or help, protection or counsel from this member, and in return were happy to provide generously for his manifold needs, he also found protection, respect, and a hearing among the more powerful, and everyone cared for these chosen men, equipped with miraculous powers, as for children of Heaven whose presence and favor spread manifold blessing abroad. Childlike faith bound men to their pronouncements. How cheerfully every man could fulfill his earthly labors when, through the agency of these holy persons, a secure future was prepared for him and every misstep forgiven, when every discolored spot in life was obliterated by them and made clean. They were the experienced helmsmen upon the great unknown sea, in whose keeping one might disdain all storms and count on a sure attainment of the coast and a landing at the world of the true home.

Before their words the wildest and most voracious propensities were obliged to yield respect and obedience. Peace proceeded from them. They preached solely love for the holy and wondrously beautiful Lady of Christendom, who, endowed with divine powers, was prepared to rescue any believer from the most dread perils. They told of celestial persons long since dead who, by virtue of adherence and loyalty to that Blessed Mother and to her divine and benevolent Child, withstood the temptation of the earthly world and achieved honors and had now become protective and beneficent powers to their living brethren, willing helpers in tribulation, intercessors for human

Christendom or Europe?

infirmities, and efficacious friends of mankind before the heavenly throne. With what serenity people used to depart from the beautiful assemblies in the mysterious churches, which were adorned with cheering pictures, filled with sweet fragrances, and animated by holy and exalting music. Therein the consecrated remains of former God-fearing men were gratefully preserved in precious reliquaries. And through them was manifest the divine goodness and omnipotence, the powerful beneficence of these happy saints, in splendid wonders and signs. In this way loving souls preserve locks of hair or bits of writing of their departed loved ones and feed the sweet flame thereby until reuniting death. With heartfelt care people used to gather from everywhere whatever had belonged to these beloved souls, and each man considered himself fortunate who was able to procure, or so much as touch, such a consoling relic. Now and again the heavenly grace seemed to have descended especially upon some strange picture or upon a grave. Thither streamed people then from all regions with lovely gifts and carried away heavenly gifts in return: peace of soul and health of body.

Assiduously this powerful peace-creating organization sought to make all men sharers in this beautiful faith and sent their colleagues into all parts of the world to proclaim everywhere the Gospel of Life and to make the Kingdom of Heaven the only kingdom on this earth. With good cause the wise Head of the Church countered insolent excrescences of human talents at the expense of the sacred sense, as well as untimely, dangerous discoveries in the area of knowledge. Thus he prevented bold thinkers from asserting publicly that the earth was an insignificant planet, for he realized that humans, together with respect for their dwelling place and their earthly homeland, would also lose respect for their heavenly home and for their race, would prefer circumscribed knowledge to infinite faith, and would become accustomed to scorning everything great and worthy of wonder and look upon these as dead legalisms. At his court assembled all the clever and reverend men in Europe. All treasures flowed thither, Jerusalem destroyed had avenged itself, and Rome itself was Jerusalem, the holy residence of divine government on earth. Princes laid their disputes before the father of Christendom, willingly laid their crowns and their splendor at his feet. Indeed, they deemed it a glory to conclude the evening of their lives as members of that high guild in godly contempla-

Christendom or Europe?

tion within solitary cloister walls. How beneficial this regimen, this arrangement was, how appropriate to the inner nature of man, was shown by the mighty upsurge of all the other human powers, the harmonious development of all capacities, the tremendous height to which individual men attained in all departments of knowledge of life and of the arts, and by the universally flourishing traffic in spiritual and earthly wares within the boundaries of Europe and outward to the most distant Indies.

Such were the fine essential characteristics of the truly Catholic or truly Christian times. For this splendid kingdom mankind was not ripe, not developed enough. It was a first love, which died away amid the press of business life, whose memory was crowded out by selfish cares, and whose bond—afterwards cried down as imposture and illusion and judged in the light of subsequent experiences—was sundered forever by a large proportion of Europeans. This great inner cleavage, which was attended by destructive wars, was a noteworthy sign of the harmfulness of culture to the sense for the Invisible, or at least of the temporary harmfulness of the culture of a certain stage. Annihilated that immortal sense cannot be, but it can be troubled, lamed, crowded out by other senses. Protracted intercourse of human beings decreases their affections, their belief in their race, and accustoms them to devoting their entire aim and endeavor solely to the means of wellbeing. Their needs and the devices for the satisfaction of their needs become more complex; and the greedy man requires so much time to get to know them and to acquire skills in them, that no time is left for the quiet composure of the spirit, for attentive observation of the inner world. In cases of conflict, present concerns seem to touch him more nearly, and thus faith and love, the fair blossoms of his youth, fall and yield place to the tarter fruits, knowledge and possessions. In late autumn one recalls the springtime as a childish dream, and with childish simplicity one hopes that the full granary will hold out forever. A certain solitariness seems to be necessary for the thriving of the higher senses, and hence a too extensive association of persons one with another will inevitably choke out many a sacred stalk and frighten away the gods who flee the unquiet tumult of distracted societies and the transactions of petty occasions.

We have, moreover, to do with times and periods, and for such, is not an oscillation, an alternation of opposing movements, essential? And is

Christendom or Europe?

limited duration not characteristic of them? Is growth and decline not their nature? But also, is not resurrection and rejuvenation in new and vigorous form to be expected with certainty of them? Progressive, ever augmenting evolutions are the stuff of history. What now does not attain fulfillment, will attain it upon a future trial or upon a reiterated one. Nothing is perishable which history has taken up. Out of untold transmutations it emerges again in ever riper forms. Christianity had once appeared in full force and splendor; down to a new world-inspiration its ruin and its Letter endured amid ever increasing feebleness and derision. Infinite inertia lay heavy upon the now safe guild of the clergy. In the feeling of its esteem and its comfort it had stopped moving, while the laity had wrested experience and erudition from its hands and had taken mighty strides ahead of it on the way to culture. In the forgetfulness of its true office, which was to be the first among men in intellect, insight, and culture, base desires had grown rank, and the vulgarity and baseness of their mode of thinking became still more repugnant because of their garb and their vocation. Thus respect and confidence, the props of this and every kingdom, fell gradually away, and therewith that guild was undone. The actual mastery of Rome had, long before the violent insurrection, silently ceased to be. Merely clever, and therefore also merely transient, measures still held the corpse of the organization together and protected it from too rapid dissolution, into which category fell, for example, primarily the abolition of marriage for the clergy—a measure which, applied analogously, could bestow a redoubtable solidity upon the parallel military caste and confer upon it long extension of life. What was more natural than that finally a mind quick to take flame should preach open rebellion against the despotic Letter of the former organization, and with all the greater success because he himself was a member of the guild.

The insurgents rightly termed themselves Protestants, for they protested solemnly against the usurpation of the conscience by an inconvenient and seemingly illegal force. For the time being they reappropriated, as though it were free, their silently surrendered right to the examination, determination, and choice of religion. They also set up a number of right principles, introduced a number of praiseworthy things, and abolished a number of pernicious laws. But they forgot the inevitable result of their procedure, they separated the inseparable, divided the indivisible Church, and sacrilegiously wrenched themselves loose from the universal Christian community, through which and in which alone was possible the true, the enduring rebirth. The condition of religious anarchy must not be more than transitory, because there remains constantly operative and valid the reason for dedicating a number of people exclusively to this high vocation and for making this number of people independent of temporal force with regard to these affairs. The establishment of consistories and the retention of a kind of clergy was of no help toward this requirement and was no adequate substitute for it. Unfortunately the princes had intruded themselves into this schism and many of them used these contentions for the re-enforcement and extension of their sovereign power and incomes. They were happy to be exempt from that former high influence and now took the new consistories under their paternalistic protection and guidance. They were most zealously concerned with preventing the total unification of the Protestant churches, and thus religion was irreligiously contained within the boundaries of states, whereby was laid the foundation for the gradual undermining of cosmopolitan religious interest. Thus religion lost its great political influence for the creation of peace and its proper role as unifying, individualizing principle, the role of Christendom. Religious peace was settled according to thoroughly erroneous principles antithetical to religion, and by the continuation of so-called Protestantism something entirely contradictory—a revolutionary regime—was declared perpetual.

Meanwhile, at the foundation of Protestantism there lies by no means merely that pure concept. Rather, Luther treated Christianity quite arbitrarily, misjudged its spirit, introduced another Letter and another religion, namely the holy universal validity of the Bible, and therewith unfortunately was injected into religious affairs a different, highly alien, worldly science—philosophy—whose corrosive influence becomes henceforth unmistakable. Out of a dim perception of this error he was himself elevated by a large proportion of Protestants to the rank of evangelist and his translation canonized.

This choice was highly injurious to the religious sense, for nothing so crushes its sensitivity as the Letter. In the previous situation this latter could never have become so harmful, considering the large compass, the flexibility, and the copious matter of the Catholic faith, as well as the esotericizing of the Bible and the sacred power of the councils and of the spiritual Head. But now these counterforces were abrogated, the absolute accessibility of the Bible to the people was asserted, and now the inadequate contents, the rough, abstract sketch of religion in these books, became all the more obvious and for the spirit of holiness infinitely weighed down free animation, penetration, and revelation.

Hence the history of Protestantism shows us no great and splendid manifestations of the supernatural any more. Only its inception gleams through a transitory blaze of heaven, and soon thereafter the desiccation of the spirit of holiness is already evident. The worldly has gained the upper hand. The sense for art suffers kindredwise. Only rarely does a genuine, eternal spark of life leap forth here and there and a small congregation form. It expires and the congregation dissolves again and drifts with the current. Such were Zinzendorf, Jakob Böhme, and others. The moderates get the upper hand, and the era feeds on a total atony of the higher organs, on the period of practical disbelief. With the Reformation, Christendom came to an end. From then on there was no such thing anymore. Catholics and Protestants or Reformed stood further apart from one another in sectarian division than from

Mohammedans and heathens. The remaining Catholic states went on vegetating, not without imperceptibly feeling the harmful influence of the neighboring Protestant states. Modern politics first developed at this point in time, and individual powerful states sought to take over the vacant universal Chair, which had been transformed into a throne.

To most princes it seemed a humiliation to be inconvenienced for a powerless cleric. For the first time they felt the weight of their physical power on earth, beheld the heavenly powers idle before offense to their representatives, and now sought gradually and without fuss to cast off the burdensome Roman yoke from subjects of theirs who still inclined zealously to the Pope, and to make themselves independent on earth. Their uneasy consciences were set at rest by clever soul-keepers who had nothing to lose if their spiritual children arrogated to themselves the control of church property.

To the good fortune of the old organization there now advanced a newly arisen order on which the dying spirit of the hierarchy seemed to have poured out its uttermost gifts, which equipped the old with new strength, and which applied itself with marvelous insight and perseverance, more astutely than had ever happened before, to the Papal kingdom and its mightier regeneration. No such society had ever been met with before in world history. Not even the ancient Roman senate had devised plans for world conquest with greater certainty of success. No one had with greater sagacity yet contemplated the execution of a greater idea. This society will ever be a model of all societies that feel organic desire for infinite expansion and everlasting duration—but also a proof forever that unguarded time alone undoes the cleverest enterprises and that the natural growth of the entire species incessantly suppresses the artificial growth of any subsection. All that is specialized unto itself has its own measure of ability; only the capacity of the race is infinite. All projects must fail which are not projects fully consonant with all the natural inclinations of the race. This society becomes still more noteworthy as mother of the so-called secret societies, a growth still unripe but surely of genuine historical importance. The new Lutheranism—not Protestantism—surely could not have a more dangerous rival. All the magic of the Catholic faith became still more potent beneath its hand. The treasures of the sciences flowed back into its cells. What had been lost in Europe they sought to regain multifold in other continents, in the furthest Occident and Orient, and to acquire and vindicate the apostolic dignity and vocation. Nor did they lag in their efforts for popularity, and they well realized how much Luther had owed to his demagogic arts, his study of the common folk. Everywhere they instituted schools, penetrated confessionals, assumed professorial chairs, and engaged the presses, became poets and sages, ministers and martyrs, and in their tremendous expansion from America across Europe to China remained in the most extraordinary agreement as to deed and doctrine. From their schools they recruited with wise selection for their order. Against the Lutherans they preached with devastating zeal and sought to make the cruelest extermination of these heretics, as actual confederates of the devil, the most urgent obligation of Catholic Christendom. To them alone the Catholic states, and in particular the Papal See, owed their long survival of the Reformation, and who knows how old the world would still look if weak leaders, jealousy of princes and other clerical orders, court intrigues, and other odd circumstances had not checked their bold course and with them had not all but wiped out this last bulwark of the Catholic organization. It is sleeping now, this

Christendom or Europe?

dread order, in wretched form on the outskirts of Europe. Perhaps from thence, like the nation that is sheltering it, it will someday spread abroad with new force over its old homeland, perhaps under a different name.

The Reformation was a sign of its time. It was significant for all Europe, even if it had openly broken forth only in truly free Germany. The good minds of all nations had secretly come of age and in the illusory feeling of their vocation revolted the more sharply against obsolete constraint. The erudite is by instinct the enemy of the clergy according to the old order. The erudite and the clerical classes, once they are separated, must war to the death, for they strive for one and the same position. This separation advanced ever further, and the erudite gained the more ground the more the history of European humanity approached the age of triumphant erudition, whereas knowledge and faith entered into more decisive opposition. It was to faith that people looked to find the cause of the general impasse, and this they hoped to obviate by keen knowledge. Everywhere the sense for the holy suffered from the manifold persecutions of its previous form, its former personality. The end product of the modern manner of thinking was termed "philosophy," and under that head was reckoned everything that was opposed to the old, hence primarily every objection against religion. The initial personal hatred of the Catholic faith passed gradually over into hatred of the Bible, of the Christian faith, and finally of religion in general. Still further, the hatred of religion extended itself quite naturally and consistently to all objects of enthusiasm. It made imagination and emotion heretical, as well as morality and the love of art, the future and the past. With some difficulty it placed man first in the order of created things, and reduced the infinite creative music of the universe to the monotonous clatter of a monstrous mill, which, driven by the stream of chance and floating thereon, was supposed to be a mill in the abstract, without Builder or Miller, in fact an actual *perpetuum mobile*, a mill that milled of itself.

One enthusiasm was generously left to poor mankind and, as a touchstone of supreme culture, was made indispensable to every shareholder in it—enthusiasm for this grand and splendid "philosophy" and more particularly for its priests and initiates. France was fortunate enough to become the womb and the seat of this new faith, which was pasted together out of pure knowledge. Yet,

Christendom or Europe?

decried as poetry was in this new church, there were nevertheless some poets in its midst who, for the sake of effect, still made use of the old adornments and of the old light, though in so doing they ran the risk of setting the new world system on fire with the old flame. Shrewder members, however, knew how to pour cold water at once upon such listeners as had waxed warm. The members were tirelessly busy cleaning the poetry of Nature, the earth, the human soul, and the branches of learning—obliterating every trace of the holy, discrediting by sarcasm the memory of all ennobling events and persons, and stripping the world of all colorful ornament. The Light, by virtue of its mathematical submissiveness and its insolence, had become their favorite. They rejoiced that it yielded to refraction sooner than to play with colors, and thus they took from it the name of their great undertaking: Enlightenment. In Germany this undertaking was prosecuted even more thoroughly. The educational system was reformed. An attempt was made to impart to the old religion a more modern, more rational, more general meaning by carefully washing it clean of all that was marvelous or mysterious. The whole of scholarship was enlisted to cut off refuge in history, while people strove to elevate history itself to a domestic and civic portrait of manners and families. God was made into the disengaged spectator of this great, touching drama which the scholars were mounting, at the conclusion of which He was expected to entertain and solemnly admire the poets and players. By downright preference the common people were enlightened and educated to that cultivated enthusiasm, and in this way there arose a new European guild: the Lovers of Mankind and Enlighteners. What a pity that Nature remained so wondrous and incomprehensible, so poetic and infinite, in defiance of all the efforts to modernize her. If somewhere an old superstition about a higher world and the like turned up, a hue and cry was straightway raised on all sides and wherever possible the dangerous spark was quenched into ashes by "philosophy" and wit. And yet Tolerance was the watchword of the cultured, and particularly in France was reckoned synonymous with "philosophy."

This history of modern disbelief is highly significant and the key to all the tremendous phenomena of recent times. It has its first beginning in this century, especially in the latter half, and in a brief span has grown to incalculable size and diversity. A second Reformation, more comprehensive and more specifically characteristic, was

Christendom or Europe?

inevitable, and it had to strike first in that country which was most modernized and which, from lack of freedom, had lain longest in an asthenic state. The supernatural fire would long since have burst forth and set at naught the clever plans for enlightenment, had not secular pressure and influence come to the latter's support. But at that moment, when dissension arose between the erudite and the new regimes, between the enemies of religion and their whole fellowship, it necessarily emerged as a third, tone-setting, conciliating member, and this emergence must now be acknowledged by every friend thereof and proclaimed aloud, even if it should not be especially evident. That the time of resurrection has come, and that precisely those circumstances which seemed to be directed against its animation and which threatened to complete its destruction, have become the most favorable signs for its regeneration, this cannot remain in doubt to a person with a sense of history. Genuine anarchy is the creative element of religion. Out of the annihilation of all that is positive it raises its glorious head as a new creator of worlds. As though of himself, man rises toward heaven when nothing else holds him bound; the higher organs rise for the first time of their own will out of the general uniform mass and out of the total dissolution of all human abilities and powers, as the primeval seed of earthly formation. The spirit of God hovers over the waters and a heavenly island is discernible above the retreating waves as the dwelling place of the new man, as the river-bed of eternal life.

Let the true beholder contemplate calmly and dispassionately the new state-toppling era. Will not the state-toppler seem to him like Sisyphus? Now he has attained the summit of equilibrium, and already the mighty weight is rolling down the other side again. It will never remain on high unless an attraction toward heaven holds it poised on the crest. All your props are too weak if your state retains its tendency toward the earth. But link it by a higher yearning to the heights of heaven, give it a relevancy to the universe, and you will have in it a never-wearying spring, and you will see your efforts richly rewarded. I refer you to history. Search amid its instructive coherency for parallel points of time and learn to use the magic wand of analogy.

Is the Revolution to remain the French one, as the Reformation was the Lutheran one? Is Protestantism once again, contrary to nature, to be fixed as a revolutionary regime? Shall the Letter make way for the Letter? Are you seeking the seed-germ of deterioration in the old order too, in the old spirit? And do you imagine yourselves on a better tack toward the understanding of a better spirit? O would that the spirit of spirits filled you and you would desist from this foolish effort to mold history and mankind and to give it your direction! Is it not independent, not self-empowered, as well as infinitely lovable and prophetic? To study it, to follow after it, to learn from it, to keep step with it, to follow in faith its promises and hints—of these things no one thinks.

In France a great deal has been done for religion by withdrawing its right of citizenship and leaving it solely the right of tenancy in the household, and this not in One Person but in all its countless individual forms. As a strange, unprepossessing waif it must first win hearts again and be universally loved before it can be publicly worshiped again and be drawn into secular matters for friendly advice and the harmonizing of spirits. Historically noteworthy remains the attempt of that great iron mask which, under the name of Robespierre, sought in religion the mid-point and the strength of the Republic. Likewise the insensibility with which theophilanthropy, that mystique of modern Enlightenment, was taken up.

Likewise the new conquests of the Jesuits. Likewise the approach to the Orient through recent political circumstances.

Of the other European countries besides Germany it may be prophesied only that, with *peace*, a new and higher religious life will begin to pulse within them and that this will soon consume all other secular interests. In Germany, on the other hand, the traces of a new world can already be demonstrated with total certainty. Germany is proceeding, at slow but sure pace, ahead of the other European countries. While the latter are occupied with war, speculation, and partisan spirit, the German is developing himself with all industry into a partaker in a higher epoch of culture, and this advance cannot fail to give him a great advantage over the others in the course of time. In learning and in the arts one detects a mighty ferment. Infinitely vast intelligence is being developed. Requisition is being made from new and fresh lodes of ore. Never was learning in better hands, never did it arouse greater expectations. The most varied aspects of objects are being explored. Nothing is being left unstirred, unjudged, unexamined. Everything is being worked. Writers are becoming more individualized and more powerful. Every old monument of history, every art, every branch of knowledge is finding friends, is being embraced with new love and made fruitful. A versatility without parallel, a wonderful profundity, a splendid polish, comprehensive knowledge, and a rich and mighty imagination are to be found on this side and on that side, often daringly combined. A tremendous intimation of the creative will, of the boundlessness, of the infinite multiplicity, of the sacred particularity and universal capability of the inner man seems everywhere to be astir. Awakened from the morning dream of helpless childhood, a section of the race is exerting its first powers against serpents that entwine its cradle and seek to filch from it the use of its limbs. All these things are still only intimations, incoherent and raw, but to the historical eye they give evidence of a universal individuality, a new history, a new mankind, the sweetest embrace of a young and surprised Church and a loving God, and the fervent reception of a new Messiah within its thousand members. Who does not, with sweet shame, feel himself pregnant? The newborn child will be the image of his father, a new Golden Age, with dark and infinite eyes, an Age prophetic, wonder-working, miraculously healing, comforting, and kindling eternal life—a great Age of reconciliation, a Savior who, like a good spirit, is at home among men, believed in though not seen, visible under countless forms to believers, consumed as bread and wine, embraced as a bride, breathed as air, heard as word and song, and with heavenly delight accepted as death into the core of the subsiding body amid the supreme pangs of love.

We now stand high enough to smile amicably at those previous ages mentioned above and also to recognize remarkable crystallizations of historical matter even amid those odd follies. Gratefully we wish to press the hands of those scholars and "philosophers." For that illusion had to be exhausted for the benefit of posterity and the scientific aspect of things had to be validated. Lovelier and more colorful stands poetry, like an India adorned, opposed to the cold, lifeless peak of that closed-room intelligence. In order that India may be so warm and resplendent in the middle of the globe, it was necessary that a cold and rigid sea, dead cliffs, fog instead of starry sky, and a long night should make both extremes inhospitable. The profound significance of mechanics lay heavy upon those anchorites in the deserts of Reason. The charm of first insight overwhelmed them; the old took its revenge upon them. To the first awareness of self they sacrificed the holiest and most beautiful things in the world in astounding denial, and they were the first to acknowledge anew through deeds and to proclaim the sacredness of Nature, the infinitude of Art, the ineluctability of knowledge, respect for the secular, and the omnipresence of the genuinely historical; and they were the first to put an end to a higher, more universal, and more terrible dominion of ghosts than they themselves had thought.

Only through more exact knowledge of religion will the dread begotten of religious sleep, those dreams and deliria of the sacred organ, be better judged, and only then will the importance of that gift be properly appreciated. Where no gods are, ghosts prevail, and the actual development time of European ghosts—and this fairly completely accounts for their forms—was the period of transition from Greek doctrines of gods into Christianity. Come, therefore, you Lovers of Mankind and encyclopedists, into the pacific lodge and receive the fraternal kiss, cast off the grey net, and with youthful love behold the wondrous splendor of Nature, of History, and of Mankind. I shall lead you to a brother, and he shall speak with you so that your hearts shall leap up, and so that you shall clothe your dead, beloved intuition with a new body, and so that you shall embrace again and recognize what hovered before you and what the sluggish earthly intelligence could not grasp for you.

This brother is the heartbeat of the new era. Whoever has felt it no longer doubts of the era's coming, and with sweet pride in his contemporaneity steps forth even from among the multitude to the new band of disciples. He has made a new veil for the Holy One, which, clinging, betrays the heavenly mold of her limbs and yet conceals her more decorously than any other. The veil is to the virgin what the mind is to the body, its indispensable organ, whose folds are the letters of her sweet annunciation. The infinite play of the folds is a cipher-music, for speech is too wooden and too insolent for the virgin: her lips open only for song. To me it is nothing less than the solemn call to a new primeval assembly, the mighty wingstroke of a passing angelic herald. These are the first pangs: let everyone prepare for delivery in birth!

The highest development in natural philosophy is now at hand and we can the more easily now survey the learned guild. The indigence of the external sciences had become the more evident in recent times the more familiar we became with them. Nature began to look ever more indigent,

Christendom or Europe?

and, accustomed to the brilliance of our discoveries, we saw more plainly that it was only a borrowed light and that with known instruments and by known methods we would not find and construe the essential thing we sought. Each investigator had to confess that one branch of knowledge was nothing without the others, and thus there arose attempts at mystification in the branches of knowledge; the wayward soul of philosophy, demonstrated as a mere scientific element, fell into place in a symmetrical basic figure of the sciences. Others brought the concrete sciences into new circumstances, promoted a lively interchange among them, and tried to set clear their natural historical classification. And so it continues, and it is easy to estimate how favorable must be this association with both the external and internal worlds, with the higher cultivation of the intellect, with the knowledge of the former and the stimulation and culture of the latter, and how under these circumstances the weather must clear and the old heaven must again come into view, and with it the yearning for it, the living astronomy.

Now let us turn to the political spectacle of our time. The old world and the new world are engaged in battle. The defectiveness and short-

CHRISTENDOM OR EUROPE?

comings of the organization of states up to now have become apparent in dreadful phenomena. What if here, too, as in the branches of knowledge, closer and more multiple connections and contacts of European states were the primary historical goal of war? What if a new stirring of hitherto slumbering Europe were to come into play? What if Europe were to reawaken and a state of states, a political theory of knowledge, were to confront us! Might perhaps hierarchy, that symmetrical basic figure of states, be the principle of unification of states, as the intellectual concept of the political ego? It is impossible for secular forces to put themselves into equilibrium; only a third element, which is at once secular and super-worldly, can solve that problem. Between the conflicting powers themselves no peace can be established. All peace is mere illusion, mere truce. From the standpoint of cabinets or the common consciousness, no unification is conceivable. Both parties have great and urgent claims and must make them, driven as they are by the spirit of the world and of mankind. Both are indestructible powers in the heart of man: on the one side reverence for antiquity, dependence upon historical system, love for the monuments of ancestors and of the ancient and glorious family of the state,

Christendom or Europe?

and joy in obedience; on the other side delightsome sensation of freedom, unlimited expectation of tremendous provinces of activity, pleasure in things new and young, effortless contact with all members of the state, pride in the universal validity of man, joy in one's personal rights and in the property of the whole, and the powerful feeling of citizenship. Let neither of these two hope to destroy the other. All conquests are meaningless here, for the inner capital of every kingdom lies not behind earthwalls and is not to be taken by siege.

Who knows whether there has been enough of war? But it will never come to an end unless someone grasps the palm branch, which a spiritual power alone can proffer. Blood will wash over Europe until the nations perceive the fearful madness which is driving them about in a circle; until, arrested by holy music and soothed, they approach former alters in multi-hued fusion and undertake works of peace; until a great feast of love is celebrated as a festival of peace amid hot tears upon smoking battlefields. Only religion can waken Europe again, and reassure the peoples, and install Christendom with new splendor visibly on earth in its old peace-establishing office.

Do nations have about them everything of the

human being—except his heart?—except his holy organ? Will they not become friends, as men do, beside the coffins of their loves? Will they not forget all that is hostile when heavenly compassion speaks to them?—and one misfortune, one sorrow, one emotion has filled their eyes with tears? Will sacrifice and surrender not seize them with irresistible force? And will they not yearn to be friends and allies?

Where is that old, dear faith, which alone can render blessed, in God's government on earth? Where is that heavenly trust of humans in one another, that sweet piety amid the outpouring of a God-inspired heart, that all-embracing spirit of Christendom?

Christianity is of a threefold form. One is the creative element of religion, the joy in all religion. One is intercession in and of itself, faith in the universal capacity of all earthly things to be the bread and wine of eternal life. One is faith in Christ, His Mother, and the Saints. Choose which one you will. Choose all three, it makes no difference. You will thereby become Christians and members of a single, eternal, ineffable community.

Applied, vitalized Christianity was the old Catholic faith, the last of these forms. Its omni-

Christendom or Europe?

presence in life, its love of art, its profound humanity, the inviolability of its marriages, its communicativeness benevolent to man, its joy in poverty, obedience, and loyalty, render it unmistakable as genuine religion and comprise the basic features of its system.

It had been purified in the river of eras. In intimate and indissoluble combination with the other two forms of Christianity it will ever make fortunate this earth. Its accidental form is as good as annihilated.

The old Papacy lies in its grave and Rome for the second time has become a ruin. Shall Protestantism not cease at last and make way for a new, enduring Church? The other continents await Europe's reconciliation and resurrection in order to join with it and become fellow-citizens of the heavenly kingdom. Should there not be presently once again in Europe a host of truly holy spirits? Should not all those truly related in religion become full of yearning to behold heaven on earth? And should they not gladly join together and begin songs of holy choirs?

Christendom must come alive again and be effective, and, without regard to national boundaries, again form a visible Church which will take into its bosom all souls athirst for the supernatural, and willingly become the mediatrix between the old world and the new.

It must once again pour out the cornucopia of blessing over peoples. From the holy womb of a venerable European Council shall Christendom arise, and the task of awakening will be prosecuted according to a comprehensive divine plan. Then no one will protest any longer against Christian and secular compulsion, for the essence of the Church will be true freedom, and all necessary reforms will be carried out under its guidance as a peaceful and formal state process.

When and when sooner? The question is not to be asked. Patience only! It will, it must come, that sacred time of endless peace when the new Jerusalem will be the capital of the world. Until then be cheerful and courageous amid the dangers of the time. Partakers of my faith, proclaim with word and deed the divine Gospel, and to the veritable and everlasting Faith remain true unto death.

The Spiritual Songs of Novalis
Translated by George MacDonald

I.

Without thee, what were life or being!
Without thee, what had I not grown!
From fear and anguish vainly fleeing,
I in the world had stood alone;
For all I loved could trust no shelter;
The future a dim gulf had lain;
And when my heart in tears did welter,
To whom had I poured out my pain?

Consumed in love and longing lonely
Each day had worn the night's dull face;
With hot tears I had followed only
Afar life's wildly rushing race.
No rest for me, tumultuous driven!
A hopeless sorrow by the hearth!—
Who, that had not a friend in heaven,
Could to the end hold out on earth?

But if his heart once Jesus bareth,
And I of him right sure can be,

CHRISTENDOM OR EUROPE?

How soon a living glory scareth
The bottomless obscurity!
Manhood in him first man attaineth;
His fate in Him transfigured glows;
On freezing Iceland India gaineth,
And round the loved one blooms and blows.

Life grows a twilight softly stealing;
The world speaks all of love and glee;
For every wound grows herb of healing,
And every heart beats full and free.
I, his ten thousand gifts receiving,
Humble like him, his knees embrace;
Sure that we share his presence living
When two are gathered in one place.

Forth, forth to all highways and hedges!
Compel the wanderers to come in;
Stretch out the hand that good will pledges,
And gladly call them to their kin.
See heaven high over earth up-dawning!
In faith we see it rise and spread:
To all with us one spirit owning—
To them with us 'tis openéd.

An ancient, heavy guilt-illusion
Haunted our hearts, a changeless doom;
Blindly we strayed in night's confusion;

The Spiritual Songs of Novalis

Gladness and grief alike consume.
Whate'er we did, some law was broken!
Mankind appeared God's enemy;
And if we thought the heavens had spoken,
They spoke but death and misery.

The heart, of life the fountain swelling—
An evil creature lay therein;
If more light shone into our dwelling,
More unrest only did we win.
Down to the earth an iron fetter
Fast held us, trembling captive crew;
Fear of Law's sword, grim Death the whetter,
Did swallow up hope's residue.

Then came a saviour to deliver—
A Son of Man, in love and might!
A holy fire, of life all-giver,
He in our hearts has fanned alight.
Then first heaven opened—and, no fable,
Our own old fatherland we trod!
To hope and trust we straight were able,
And knew ourselves akin to God.

Then vanished Sin's old spectre dismal;
Our every step grew glad and brave.
Best natal gift, in rite baptismal,

Their own faith men their children gave.
Holy in him, Life since hath floated,
A happy dream, through every heart;
We, to his love and joy devoted,
Scarce know the moment we depart.

Still standeth, in his wondrous glory,
The holy loved one with his own;
His crown of thorns, his faithful story
Still move our hearts, still make us groan.
Whoso from deadly sleep will waken,
And grasp his hand of sacrifice,
Into his heart with us is taken,
To ripen a fruit of Paradise.

The Spiritual Songs of Novalis

II.

Dawn, far eastward, on the mountain!
Gray old times are growing young:
From the flashing colour-fountain
I will quaff it deep and long!—
Granted boon to Longing's long privation!
Sweet love in divine transfiguration!

Comes at last, our old Earth's native,
All-Heaven's one child, simple, kind!
Blows again, in song creative,
Round the earth a living wind;
Blows to clear new flames that rush together
Sparks extinguished long by earthly
weather.

Everywhere, from graves upspringing,
Rises new-born life, new blood!
Endless peace up to us bringing,
Dives he underneath life's flood;
Stands in midst, with full hands, eyes caress-
ing—
Hardly waits the prayer to grant the bless-
ing.

Let his mild looks of invading
Deep into thy spirit go;
By his blessedness unfading

CHRISTENDOM OR EUROPE?

Thou thy heart possessed shalt know.
Hearts of all men, spirits all, and senses
Mingle, and a new glad dance commences.

Grasp his hands with boldness yearning;
Stamp his face thy heart upon;
Turning toward him, ever turning,
Thou, the flower, must face thy sun.
Who to him his heart's last fold unfoldeth,
True as wife's his heart for ever holdeth.

Ours is now that Godhead's splendour
At whose name we used to quake!
South and north, its breathings tender
Heavenly germs at once awake!
Let us then in God's full garden labour,
And to every bud and bloom be neighbour!

III.

Who in his chamber sitteth lonely,
  And weepeth heavy, bitter tears;
To whom in doleful colours, only
  Of want and woe, the world appears;

Who of the Past, gulf-like receding,
  Would search with questing eyes the core,
Down into which a sweet woe, pleading,
  Wiles him from all sides evermore—

As if a treasure past believing
  Lay there below, for him high-piled,
After whose lock, with bosom heaving,
  He breathless grasps in longing wild:

He sees the Future, waste and arid,
  In hideous length before him stretch;
About he roams, alone and harried,
  And seeks himself, poor restless wretch!—

I fall upon his bosom, tearful:
  I once, like thee, with woe was wan;
But I grew well, am strong and cheerful,
  And know the eternal rest of man.

CHRISTENDOM OR EUROPE?

Thou too must find the one consoler
  Who inly loved, endured, and died—
Even for them that wrought his dolour
  With thousand-fold rejoicing died.

He died—and yet, fresh each to-morrow,
  His love and him thy heart doth hold;
Thou mayst, consoled for every sorrow,
  Him in thy arms with ardour fold.

New blood shall from his heart be driven
  Through thy dead bones like living wine;
And once thy heart to him is given,
  Then is his heart for ever thine.

What thou didst lose, he keeps it for thee;
  With him thy lost love thou shalt find;
And what his hand doth once restore thee,
  That hand to thee will changeless bind.

IV.

Of the thousand hours me meeting,
And with gladsome promise greeting,
  One alone hath kept its faith—
One wherein—ah, sorely grieved!—
In my heart I first perceived
  Who for us did die the death.

All to dust my world was beaten;
As a worm had through them eaten
  Withered in me bud and flower;
All my life had sought or cherished
In the grave had sunk and perished;
  Pain sat in my ruined bower.

While I thus, in silence sighing,
Ever wept, on Death still crying,
  Still to sad delusions tied,
All at once the night was cloven,
From my grave the stone was hoven,
  And my inner doors thrown wide.

Whom I saw, and who the other,
Ask me not, or friend or brother!—
  Sight seen once, and evermore!
Lone in all life's eves and morrows,
This hour only, like my sorrows,
  Ever shines my eyes before.

V.

If I him but have,[1]
  If he be but mine,
If my heart, hence to the grave,
  Ne'er forgets his love divine—
Know I nought of sadness,
Feel I nought but worship, love, and gladness.

If I him but have,
  Pleased from all I part;
Follow, on my pilgrim staff,
  None but him, with honest heart;
Leave the rest, nought saying,
On broad, bright, and crowded highways straying.

If I him but have,
  Glad to sleep I sink;
From his heart the flood he gave
  Shall to mine be food and drink;
And, with sweet compelling,
Mine shall soften, deep throughout it welling.

---

[1] Here I found the double or feminine rhyme impossible without the loss of the far more precious simplicity of the original, which could be retained only by a literal translation.

The Spiritual Songs of Novalis

If I him but have,
  Mine the world I hail;
Happy, like a cherub grave
  Holding back the Virgin's veil:
I, deep sunk in gazing,
Hear no more the Earth or its poor praising.

Where I have but him
  Is my fatherland;
Every gift a precious gem
  Come to me from his own hand!
Brothers long deploréd,
Lo, in his disciples, all restoréd!

VI.

My faith to thee I break not,
  If all should faithless be,
That gratitude forsake not
  The world eternally.
For my sake Death did sting thee
  With anguish keen and sore;
Therefore with joy I bring thee
  This heart for evermore.

Oft weep I like a river
  That thou art dead, and yet
So many of thine thee, Giver
  Of life, life-long forget!
By love alone posseséd,
  Such great things thou hast done!
But thou art dead, O Blessed,
  And no one thinks thereon!

Thou stand'st with love unshaken
  Ever by every man;
And if by all forsaken,
  Art still the faithful one.
Such love must win the wrestle;
  At last thy love they'll see,
Weep bitterly, and nestle
  Like children to thy knee.

The Spiritual Songs of Novalis

>Thou with thy love hast found me!
> O do not let me go!
>Keep me where thou hast bound me
> Till one with thee I grow.
>My brothers yet will waken,
> One look to heaven will dart—
>Then sink down, love-o'ertaken,
> And fall upon thy heart.

VII.

HYMN.
Few understand
The mystery of Love,
Know insatiableness,
And thirst eternal.
Of the Last Supper
The divine meaning
Is to the earthly senses a riddle;
But he that ever
From warm, beloved lips,
Drew breath of life;
In whom the holy glow
Ever melted the heart in trembling waves;
Whose eye ever opened so
As to fathom
The bottomless deeps of heaven—
Will eat of his body
And drink of his blood
Everlastingly.
Who of the earthly body
Has divined the lofty sense?
Who can say
That he understands the blood?
One day all is body,
One body:
In heavenly blood
Swims the blissful two.

Oh that the ocean
Were even now flushing!
And in odorous flesh
The rock were upswelling!
Never endeth the sweet repast;
Never doth Love satisfy itself;
Never close enough, never enough its own,
Can it *have* the beloved!
By ever tenderer lips
Transformed, the Partaken
Goes deeper, grows nearer.
Pleasure more ardent
Thrills through the soul;
Thirstier and hungrier
Becomes the heart;
And so endureth Love's delight
From everlasting to everlasting.
Had the refraining
Tasted but once,
All had they left
To set themselves down with us
To the table of longing
Which will never be bare;
Then had they known Love's
Infinite fullness,
And commended the sustenance
Of body and blood.

VIII.

Weep I must—my heart runs over:
Would he once himself discover—
  If but once, from far away!
Holy sorrow! still prevailing
Is my weeping, is my wailing:
  Would that I were turned to clay!

Evermore I hear him crying
To his Father, see him dying:
  Will this heart for ever beat!
Will my eyes in death close never?
Weeping all into a river
  Were a bliss for me too sweet!

Hear I none but me bewailing?
Dies his name an echo failing?
  Is the world at once struck dead?
Shall I from his eyes, ah! never
More drink love and life for ever?
  Is he now for always dead?

Dead? What means that sound of dolour?
Tell me, tell me thou, a scholar,
  What it means, that word so grim.
He is silent; all turn from me!

The Spiritual Songs of Novalis

No one on the earth will show me
  Where my heart may look for him!

Earth no more, whate'er befall me,
Can to any gladness call me!
  She is but one dream of woe!
I too am with him departed:
Would I lay with him, still-hearted,
  In the region down below!

Hear, me, hear, his and my father!
My dead bones, I pray thee, gather
  Unto his—and soon, I pray!
Grass his hillock soon will cover,
Soon the wind will wander over,
  Soon his form will fade away.

If his love they once perceived,
Soon, soon all men had believed,
  Letting all things else go by!
Lord of love him only owning,
All would weep with me bemoaning,
  And in bitter woe would die!

IX.

He lives! he's risen from the dead!
  To every man I shout;
His presence over us is spread,
  Goes with us in and out.

To each I say it; each apace
  His comrades telleth too—
That straight will dawn in every place
  The heavenly kingdom new.

Now, to the new mind, first appears
  The world a fatherland;
A new life men receive, with tears
  Of rapture, from his hand.

Down into deepest gulfs of sea
  Grim Death hath sunk away;
And now each man, with holy glee,
  Can face his coming day.

The darksome road that he hath gone
  Leads out on heaven's floor;
Who heeds the counsel of the Son
  Enters the Father's door.

The Spiritual Songs of Novalis

Down here weeps no one any more
  For friend that shuts his eyes;
For, soon or late, the parting sore
  Will change to glad surprise.

And now to every friendly deed
  Each heart will warmer glow;
For many a fold the fresh-sown seed
  In lovelier fields will blow.

He lives—will sit beside our hearths,
  The greatest with the least;
Therefore this day shall be our Earth's
  Glad Renovation-feast.

X.

The times are all so wretched!
  The heart so full of cares!
The future, far outstretched,
  A spectral horror wears.

Wild terrors creep and hover
  With foot so ghastly soft!
Our souls black midnights cover
  With mountains piled aloft.

Firm props like reeds are waving;
  For trust is left no stay;
Our thoughts, like whirlpool raving,
  No more the will obey!

Frenzy, with eye resistless,
  Decoys from Truth's defence;
Life's pulse is flagging listless,
  And dull is every sense.

Who hath the cross upheavéd
  To shelter every soul?
Who lives, on high receivéd,
  To make the wounded whole?

Go to the tree of wonder;
  Give silent longing room:
Issuing flames asunder
  Thy bad dream will consume.

Draws thee an angel tender
  In safety to the strand:
Lo, at thy feet in splendour
  Lies spread the Promised Land!

XI.

I know not what were left to draw me,
  Had I but him who is my bliss;
If still his eye with pleasure saw me,
  And, dwelling with me, me would miss.

So many search, round all ways going,
  With face distorted, anxious eye,
Who call themselves the wise and knowing,
  Yet ever pass this treasure by!

One man believes that he has found it,
  And what he has is nought but gold;
One takes the world by sailing round it:
  The deed recorded, all is told!

One man runs well to gain the laurel;
  Another, in Victory's fane a niche:
By different Shows in bright apparel
  All are befooled, not one made rich!

Hath He not then to you appearéd?
  Have ye forgot Him turning wan
Whose side for love of us was spearéd—
  The scorned, rejected Son of Man?

The Spiritual Songs of Novalis

Of Him have you not read the story—
  Heard one poor word upon the wind?
What heavenly goodness was his glory,
  Or what a gift he left behind?

How he descended from the Father,
  Of loveliest mother infant grand?
What Word the nations from him gather?
  How many bless his healing hand?

How, thereto urged by mere love, wholly
  He gave himself to us away,
And down in earth, foundation lowly,
  First stone of God's new city, lay?

Can such news fail to touch us mortals?
  Is not to know the man pure bliss?
Will you not open all your portals
  To him who closed for you the abyss?

Will you not let the world go faring?
  For Him your dearest wish deny?
To him alone your heart keep baring,
  Who you has shown such favour high?

Hero of love, oh, take me, take me!
  Thou art my life! my world! my gold!

CHRISTENDOM OR EUROPE?

Should every earthly thing forsake me,
  I know who will me scatheless hold!

I see Thee my lost loves restoring!
  True evermore to me thou art!
Low at thy feet heaven sinks adoring,
  And yet thou dwellest in my heart!

XII.

Earth's Consolation, why so slow?
Thy inn is ready long ago;
Each lifts to thee his hungering eyes,
And open to thy blessing lies.

O Father, pour him forth with might;
Out of thine arms, oh yield him quite!
Shyness alone, sweet shame, I know,
Kept him from coming long ago!

Haste him from thine into our arm
To take him with thy breath yet warm;
Thick clouds around the baby wrap,
And let him down into our lap.

In the cool streams send him to us;
In flames let him glow tremulous;
In air and oil, in sound and dew,
Let him pierce all Earth's structure through.

So shall the holy fight be fought,
So come the rage of hell to nought;
And, ever blooming, dawn again
The ancient Paradise of men.

CHRISTENDOM OR EUROPE?

Earth stirs once more, grows green and live;
Full of the Spirit, all things strive
To clasp with love the Saviour-guest,
And offer him the mother-breast.

Winter gives way; a year new-born
Stands at the manger's altar-horn;
'Tis the first year of that new Earth
Claimed by the child in right of birth.

Our eyes they see the Saviour well,
Yet in them doth the Saviour dwell;
With flowers his head is wreathed about;
From every flower himself smiles out.

He is the star; he is the sun;
Life's well that evermore will run;
From herb, stone, sea, and light's expanse
Glimmers his childish countenance.

His childlike labour things to mend,
His ardent love will never end;
He nestles, with unconscious art,
Divinely fast to every heart.

To us a God, to himself a child,
He loves us all, self un-defiled;

Becomes our drink, becomes our food—
His dearest thanks, a heart that's good.

The misery grows yet more and more;
A gloomy grief afflicts us sore:
Keep him no longer, Father, thus;
He will come home again with us!

XIII.

When in hours of fear and failing,
  All but quite our heart despairs;
When, with sickness driven to wailing,
  Anguish at our bosom tears;
Then our loved ones we remember;
  All their grief and trouble rue;
Clouds close in on our December
  And no beam of hope shines through!

Oh but then God bends him o'er us!
  Then his love comes very near!
Long we heavenward then—before us
  Lo, his angel standing clear!
Life's cup fresh to us he reaches;
  Whispers comfort, courage new;
Nor in vain our prayer beseeches
  Rest for our beloved ones too.

XIV.

Who once hath seen thee, Mother fair,
Destruction him shall never snare;
His fear is, from thee to be parted;
He loves thee evermore, true-hearted;
Thy grace remembered is the source
Whereout springs hence his spirit's highest force.

My heart is very true to thee;
My ever failing thou dost see:
Let me, sweet mother, yet essay thee—
Give me one happy sign, I pray thee.
My whole existence rests in thee:
One moment, only one, be thou with me.

I used to see thee in my dreams,
So fair, so full of tenderest beams!
The little God in thine arms lying
Took pity on his playmate crying:
But thou with high look me didst awe,
And into clouds of glory didst withdraw.

What have I done to thee, poor wretch?
To thee my longing arms I stretch!
Are not thy holy chapels ever

CHRISTENDOM OR EUROPE?

My resting-spots in life's endeavour?
O Queen, of saints and angels blest,
This heart and life take up into thy rest!

Thou know'st that I, beloved Queen,
All thine and only thine have been!
Have I not now, years of long measure,
In silence learned thy grace to treasure?
While to myself yet scarce confest,
Even then I drew milk from thy holy breast.

Oh, countless times thou stood'st by me!
I, merry child, looked up to thee!
His hands thy little infant gave me
In sign that one day he would save me;
Thou smiledst, full of tenderness,
And then didst kiss me: oh the heavenly bliss!

Afar stands now that gladness brief;
Long have I companied with grief;
Restless I stray outside the garden!
Have I then sinned beyond thy pardon?
Childlike thy garment's hem I pull:
Oh wake me from this dream so weariful!

The Spiritual Songs of Novalis

If only children see thy face,
And, confident, may trust thy grace,
From age's bonds, oh, me deliver,
And make me thine own child for ever!
The love and truth of childhood's prime
Dwell in me yet from that same golden time.

XV.

In countless pictures I behold thee,
  O Mary, lovelily expressed,
But of them all none can unfold thee
  As I have seen thee in my breast!
I only know the world's loud splendour
  Since then is like a dream o'erblown;
And that a heaven, for words too tender,
  My quieted spirit fills alone.

www.ingramcontent.com/pod-product-compliance
Lightning Source LLC
LaVergne TN
LVHW041341080426
835512LV00006B/569